CALLING THE
WILD

Leigh Cruden Kuhn

Contents

viii Foreword

1 Chapter 1: **All Life Long**

3 Chapter 2: **Cattails**

7 Chapter 3: **The Wisdom and Wit of Horses**

11 Chapter 4: **A Whistle's Power**

15 Chapter 5: **No Ant Is an Island**

23 Chapter 6: **Considerate Snakes**

31 Chapter 7: **Home on the Range**

37 Chapter 8: **Three Coyote Stories**

45 Chapter 9: **Grin and Bear It**

57 Chapter 10: **Look Closely**

97 Chapter 11: **This Tree Is Whose Tree?**

99 Chapter 12: **Parting Words**

101 Editor's Acknowledgments

Illustrations

iv	Cougar
vii	Porcupine
6	Horse
14	Ants
22	Rattlesnake
36	Playful coyote
44	Bears
56	Cougar
59	Grouse
60	Barred owl
61	Hawk
62	Crow
63	Heron
64	Honey bee
65	Dragonfly
66	Bat
67	Dolphins
68	Manatees
69	Fish
70	Salamander
71	Beaver
72	River otter
73	Seal
74	German shepherd
75	Flubs, my sister's dog
76	Jumpers, my sister's cat
77	Two black Labs
78	Bobcat
79	Raccoon
80	Wolf
81	Bison
82	Deer

83 Boar

84 Prairie dogs

85 Wolverine

86 Weasel

87 Fisher

88 Woodchuck

89 Rats

90 Mice

91 Mole

92 Badger

93 Hare

94 Mountain goat

95 Tiger

102 Tortoise

Foreword

FOR MY SISTER LEIGH, LANDSCAPE WAS not a scenic backdrop, but a vivid foreground of consciousness. She recognized – at a level even the most sensitive nature writers don't often achieve – that each creature is an individual with its own intrinsic value and its own life to lead.

Leigh didn't generalize. She also didn't project abstract or metaphysical meanings onto her encounters. An animal was itself, not a symbol or path to something.

For decades, Leigh lived in the high desert of central Oregon, in a house she designed and built herself. It became a landscaped oasis intended not only for Leigh and her husband, but one also welcoming to wildlife. Leigh worked in wildlife research and rehab, environmental education, and animal care. Her passion for the natural world informed every meticulous line of the remarkable wildlife drawings that Leigh created over the years. Her art arose from intimate observation. This book includes some of her evocative illustrations.

The letters Leigh wrote to me were lit by the fidelity of that attention. An example from just outside her house:

"The reflecting pool continues to be a popular spot. Every evening, so far without fail, the pair of doves with one offspring sits on the same flat rock on the far side of the lip, the same rocks the golden mantles sit on too. The cottontails continue to run around the edge chasing each other. Yesterday a jackrabbit came by and ate at the grass edge. A young buck tentatively drinks in the same spot but first has to approach it several times, as if the lily pads may be predatory. Today a female western tanager tried to get a shower in the fountain spray. She managed to get a little wet and not fall in."

The high desert's community of creatures was Leigh's world. She bore witness to, supported, and protected it.

"A persistent bleeping outside my window turns out to be a recently fledged golden eagle, listing into the juniper by the deck and probably addressing a plea for assistance to an (as yet) invisible parent. I always feel like I'm eavesdropping on moments and conversations, wondering what's happening next, knowing I'll likely never know."

Animals sense intentions. Leigh's were consistently interested and selfless. Instead of the traditional human belief that nature is here simply to be enjoyed, utilized, and controlled, Leigh chose instead to listen and attend to the natural world. She cherished the wild's mystery and privacy as much as she delighted in chances for close observation of it. She didn't intrude. The wild came to her, and she never tried to tame or claim or change it. This is why, I think, so many of her experiences – even the small, daily ones – were extraordinary.

"Out at dawn, watering. The chickadees are moving from bush to trees as I advance. They perch and bathe in the avalanching droplets. This morning they were fiercely displaced by two male rufous hummingbirds. I dutifully showered them as they hovered close. Morning sun and wet feathers made them glow so intensely their radiance was blinding."

Leigh's relationship with the natural world was tremendously knowledgeable, but also intuitive and deeply felt. Occasionally, it was partisan in expression: She'd shout at ravens raiding songbird nests around her house, for instance.

In her later years, Leigh did domestic animal care in her rural area. She mainly looked after people's horses when they were away, but also tended to their dogs, cats, chickens, and so on. When I visited Leigh, I'd accompany her on her rounds. She groomed, fed, watered, and cleaned up after the horses. She walked them back and forth between stalls and pasture, and administered medications. Sometimes Leigh had to firmly work with an unruly horse (like the one who kept trying to bite me while I shoveled manure in the paddock), until calm and respect were restored.

It was amazing to watch her patience. Sometimes the challenges that arose required great courage as well as skill, stamina, and compassion. But Leigh felt her efforts were reciprocated through the gift of just being with the horses: their largeness of body and spirit, their warm, earthy scent, the shuffle of hooves stirring straw, the contented grinding of teeth on hay, the velvet noses nudging her hand, and the lambent gazes so full of heart.

I remember unpaid vigils in cold barns with ailing horses, and how Leigh patiently dropper-fed a hen with a deformed beak. My sister's sense of the animal's personality and need shone through; rapport was specific.

When the owners came home to their own cats and dogs they often grumbled that their pets preferred Leigh's company to theirs. Understandably so, considering the profound contrast in their ways of relating. It was like a magic spell broke when owners returned home. Leigh hadn't treated the animals like pets. She gave them the same courtesy and regard one would a human.

The stories in this book portray my sister's extraordinary relationship with animals. Leigh tells her stories lightly, humorously. Their significance humbly unfolds as she gives voice to the unheard, acknowledgment to the unnoticed, and affection to the unbeloved and disenfranchised.

I wish there had been time for Leigh to share more of these stories prior to her death; there was a trove of them. I wish more people had had the opportunity to go for walks with Leigh. There was something just in the way she moved in a landscape, every part of her cognizant of the terrain and what grew, slithered, burrowed, flew, marched, trotted, or abided in stillness there. She'd point out elk tracks or discourse on the growth strategies of lichen, voice reticent, gestures discreet – a singular guide into a secret world. Even her naturalist colleagues recognized this about her.

You might think you knew a place, a habitat, a species, or a web of species. But if you were lucky enough to go there with Leigh, you experienced it differently and came away from it profoundly changed. That was her gift, dedicated to the wild ones. It lives on in these stories.

LOREN CRUDEN

Chapter 1

All Life Long

W HY DO SO MANY CHILDREN'S favorite books have animals as the main characters? Why, at a very early age, do children imitate animal sounds, and laugh? Makes you wonder, right?

How many of us have horses, dogs, cats, birds, or fish as our dearest companions and often our closest, most reliable connections?

Then there are all the other creatures that live in us, around us, above and below us, often unwelcome. In fact, we target many of them, benign, helpful or pests, for instant destruction.

Earth, our island home, is also home to so many forms of life that, in all the centuries humans have existed here, it is still uncertain how many species remain unknown to us.

Our realizations about nature and life on Earth are always evolving, especially about the animal world. Not long ago, for example, it was thought that brain size denoted the level of animal intelligence. We had no clue that so-called brain functions were not limited to a single organ.

I've been on a lifelong quest, fueled by animal stories, curiosity and a varied, sometimes impenetrable environment, to understand who I am, where I belong, and who or what is everything else. In this book I've written about some of my experiences with animals. I hope they demonstrate the possibilities of the values in nature.

If you are interested, come along with me. Your stories and mine will probably intersect on many points. Let's start with animals right at home. We'll get to wilder ones later.

Chapter 2

Cattails

GROWING UP, MOST PEOPLE DON'T GET much choice in what they'd like to have as pets. Getting a horse, elephant, wolf, dolphin, rat, or such as a family pet is not likely. But for some families, a dog, parakeet, goldfish, hamster, or cat can work, and for many of us such a companion was whom we came to know and love – a companion that always listened, forgave our misdeeds without judging, and shared our lives in ways others never could.

For this book, I wasn't planning to write about domestic cats. So many people have their own neat cat stories, wonderful cat videos, silly cat jokes, precious cat companions. But cats have been on my mind. My husband, Bill, and I recently lost our two very dear cats, one unexpectedly because of a blood clot, and the other by the slow cruel slide into aging and deterioration.

Our house feels erased of life even while we still have those ghostly moments of almost catching sight of one cat or the other, sure we hear cat rustlings or a brief soft meow in the night. We had grown used to Winzer waiting at the door when he heard Bill's car coming – from several miles away. Used to having our still feral cat Hidey, a.k.a. Temmy, Tattoo, Missy Poo Poo, and Princepesa, poking her head out from beneath her hidey-hole to see if I had her comb ready for our ritual morning grooming sessions. Every cat owner has these routines of caring and connection exclusive to each cat. For us, no more.

Do you remember your first pets and still think about them from time to time?

Neither Bill nor I had pet cats when we were growing up. My family had a German shepherd. I think it was my younger brother who named her Star. She was hard to run with because, as a member in good standing of her breed, she persisted in herding us four children in whatever direction she thought we should move. She also went from bedroom to bedroom every night to make sure we were each safe in bed.

Over the years, one by one, each of us grew up and moved out. Star could count. The losses troubled her. Star's muzzle was gray, her movements stiff, her eyes failing, but she continued her rounds. Finally, it came time for my brother, the youngest, to leave home. Star turned inward, my parents said. Her health declined until she passed away.

Bill's family never had any pets. About a year after we married, I stopped at a grocery store and saw a scrum of people circled near the door. In their midst huddled a tiny gray cat. The cat saw me, raced up my jeans and clung around my neck. Now what?

Several of the people patted me on the back with versions of "Well, it's yours now; good luck," leaving me not too happy with an abandoned feline attached to my neck. The cat, who became Oscar to Bill and Buddy to me, began our forty-five years of cats. All were precious components of our family. One, two, and, briefly, three at a time.

Has your life expanded and been enriched when a cat – so independent, self-contained and highly discerning about its own interests – chose a committed relationship with you?

Chapter 3

The Wisdom and Wit of Horses

WHAT I REALIZED RIGHT OFF WHEN I BEGAN WORKING as a domestic animal caretaker was that I needed to be the boss – the leader of the pack – to provide safety and, when necessary, be the enforcer. This applied to pretty much all the domesticated species I dealt with.

What took me longer to realize was that domestic animals offer an incredible doorway into acceptance, understanding, interrelatedness, connection, friendship, respect, and even love.

Getting through that doorway requires much more than just good intentions. We have to genuinely see our commonalities.

As luck or karma would have it, my first domestic animal job was the caretaking of horses for vacationing owners. I had an affinity for horses but more than affinity was needed. The owners informed me their horses were hot-bloods. I would need to always be calm but in charge. Meaning, I couldn't let them get away with anything.

One of the horses, nicknamed Hombre, had only recently been gelded and his stallion impulses still pulsed. He and another gelding, Q, were very expensive animals with names and bloodlines known in the world of horse racing.

My specific instructions for each morning and evening included which horse should walk into the stall first and by which gate, which one received which diet, and how the food needed to be scattered or placed in certain troughs. I also needed to tape Q's front legs every morning. I had tutelage on exactly how to do this correctly.

After I passed muster on the taping, one of the owners looked at me dubiously.

"You will need to bring up your chi," she said.

At the time I had no idea what she meant, but it turns out that she gave me the most important animal caretaking advice I ever received. Your state of chi (also known as "life force," among other definitions) is crucial in dealing with almost anything in life, but especially in animal caretaking.

As the owner was giving me all these instructions, Hombre and Q trailed us about, nudging each other like kids planning ways to drive their substitute teacher crazy. Fortunately, in fact, I had been a public school substitute teacher. I knew that the students' first rule was that the substitute was never going to be treated like the authority. But the sub's first rule is to take charge immediately, as if you were going to be there indefinitely, and leave no room in anyone's mind (including your own) about who is running the show.

That seemed to work effectively with my two equine charges. Their efforts to derail me never got past half-hearted. The more calmly bossy I acted, the more relaxed and cooperative they became. Within this paradigm there was a lot of room to build trust, respect, and enjoyment among the three of us.

Horses are not only smart, they're humorous. Humor is a funny thing. That's not just a lame joke, it's a sort of definition, too. For example, Hombre and Q liked to wait for an opportunity to deftly snatch off my hat. They'd hold it high, keeping it out of my reach, and then hang it on a fence post. I laughed, appreciating the joke, and no, it didn't dim my chi.

Every morning I walked Q, on his lead rope, out to the grazing field, with Hombre falling in directly behind with no attached lead. We moved out in single file. I occasionally looked back to check on Hombre, who sometimes took the opportunity to munch on the end of Q's beautiful tail, or just hold it in his mouth. I was not always successful in deterring this habit, probably because it looked so silly it made me laugh.

The last morning of my caretaking stint with Hombre and Q started as usual, with me leading Q and Hombre following, sometimes holding the end of Q's tail. Several bike riders paused along the road to watch us. They were laughing.

I turned to check on my horse charges. I was shocked to see the end of my ponytail in Q's mouth – the three of us tail-connected.

Q's eyes shone with mischief as he looked at me. He had been so clever in making sure his stride never tugged on my ponytail. I tucked the joke – their gift of trust – in the place where precious memories are stored and kept on walking.

Chapter 4

A Whistle's Power

"TWEE-TWEE TWEE-UP" ECHOED ACROSS the field, whistling three border collies into taking positions at the heels of a small herd of sheep. Rather than shouting verbal commands to their dogs, sheepherders have devised a sophisticated series of high-pitched whistles that signal the dogs to perform complex maneuvers to move and sort sheep. In areas where sheep are a major part of farming, events that show off the nuances of such whistling – and the skill of the dogs in responding – draw crowds of contestants and spectators. It is amazing and exciting to watch. (You can do that, if not in a sheep area, on the internet.)

I would consider this one instance of calling the wild. Throw in a little mischief by jackdaws and you have the wild calling the wild.

Jackdaws are shiny black birds of the same Corvidae family as North American ravens, crows and Clark's nutcrackers, to name a few. All have garnered reputations for excellent memories, skilled tool usage of whatever is handy, and devising things to do as a group that have nothing directly to do with survival and procreation.

In some parts of the United Kingdom, jackdaws have learned to accurately mimic the pitch, timing, and nuance of sheepherders' whistles. Yes, the birds whistle commands to the dogs. Imagine the confusion! That, too, is amazing and exciting to watch, though it is hard on the sheep.

Other birds, perhaps with less of a sense of sardonic humor, whistle quite purposefully. For example: Konrad Lorenz, an Austrian pioneer in the field of animal behavior, studied communication among wild greylag geese. With scientific precision he translated the summoning call of these wild geese as: "Here I am, where are you?"

Similarly, yet underwater, bottlenose dolphins whistle quite meaningfully, according to a study by marine biologists in Scotland. When groups of the dolphins meet, each dolphin whistles in an individual way never matched or copied by the others, the scientists found. "Signature whistle exchanges are a significant part of a greeting sequence" that allows the dolphins to identify members of the same species.

And that reminds me of our family. As a pre-teen in the very early years of the 20th century, my maternal grandmother, Ruth, and her best friend came up with a secret song that originally included words to the effect of "Here I am, where are you?" that they turned into an eight-note whistled tune. Whenever either heard the tune, she was supposed to drop everything and go find the other.

Years later, my grandmother used that same tune to call home her two children. (It was a lot nicer and more subtle than yelling their names – and, as with bottlenose dolphins, individually distinctive.)

Later still, her daughter – my mother – trained me and my siblings to immediately respond to that same whistled tune. All four of us, prone to roaming independently on our versions of being in the way of the wild, needed such a keening whistle to bring us home. Like greylag geese, I'm certain each of us, now well into adulthood, would still jerk to attention in automatic response to that hundred-year-old call.

Assuming – I hope – that the whistling is not being done by a joker jackdaw.

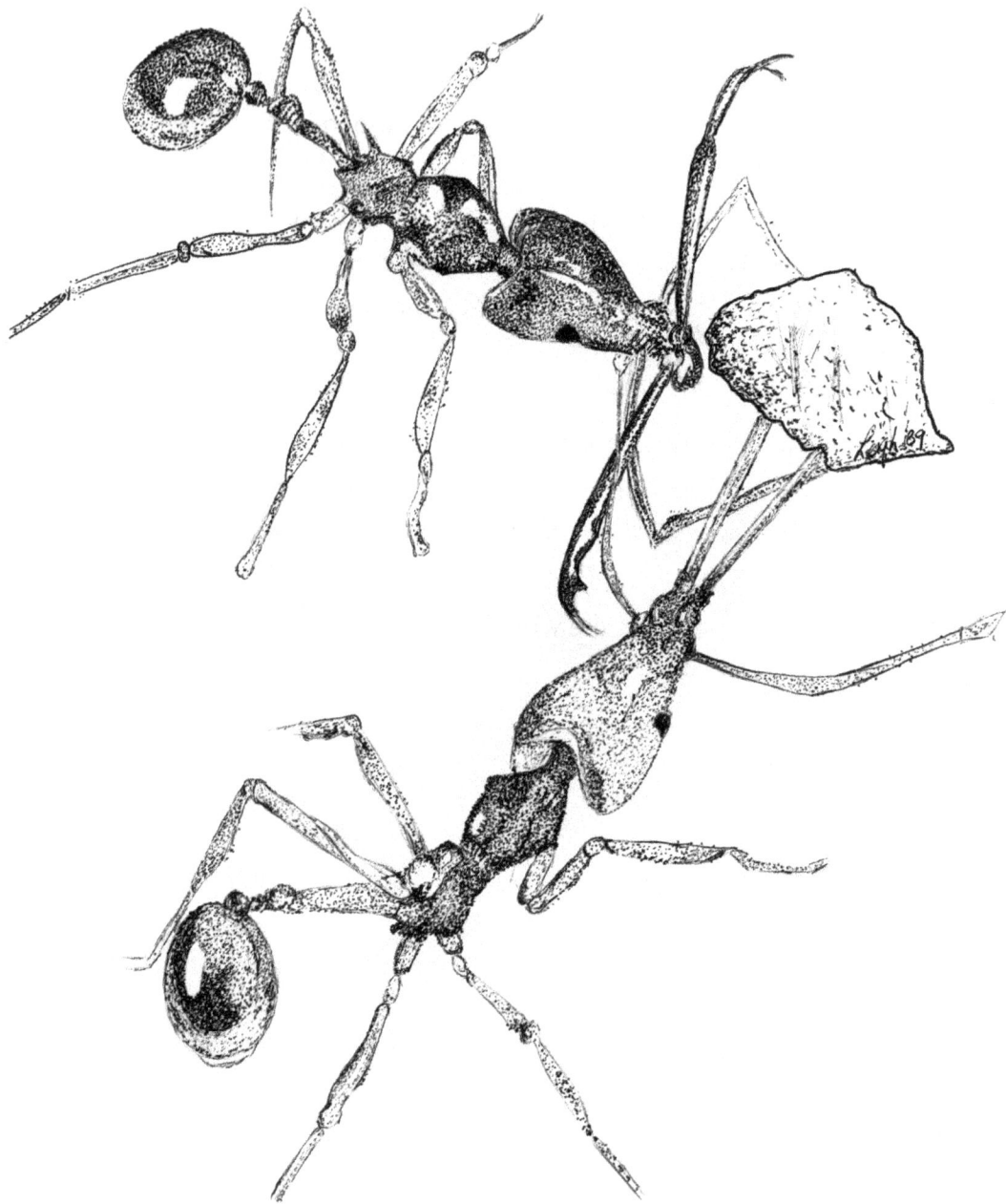

Chapter 5

No Ant Is an Island

WHATEVER CURRENT LIFE-FORMS SURVIVE Earth's changes and the impacts of our extensive occupancy here, they will surely include the ant. I've sat on a lot of dirt in many different environments on several continents, and was inevitably and swiftly joined by ants. My completely unscientific observation is that ants are virtually everywhere, except the poles. With the melting glaciers exposing bare ground, it's probably only a matter of time.

To me, ants, like lichens, have a certain impenetrable nature. I can envision the ants as robots. And like lichens, and much like us, they engage in endless warfare against each other. E.O. Wilson wrote in the prologue to his book Anthill, "Their colonies, like those of humans, are in perpetual conflict. War is a genetic imperative of most."

And: "The colonies grow and struggle and sometimes they triumph over their neighbors. Then they die, always."

Ants organize their civilizations much like we do – a strong leader, lots of busy minions who toil at their assigned jobs to keep the colony viable, and a very fierce, trained army with various levels of expertise in warfare to protect the colony and the leader.

Ants communicate by chemical scents, including leaving scent trails for other ants to follow. This is why picnic sites with discarded tidbits are suddenly swarmed by ants.

Shortly after Bill and I moved into our first house in Ohio, a sadly abused and uncared-for structure, I went into a frenzy of cleaning and making it a home. I felt like I was getting on top of things until, to my visceral shock, I discovered ants. Lots of ants – in our cereal box, in our flour bin, and just about everywhere in the kitchen that I now looked at closely.

I swept and cleaned everything again, threw out all our ant-invaded staples, and tried all the "natural" ways touted to prevent their return.

The next morning I stood in the middle of a long single-file line of marching ants. My feet were only a small deviation in their orderly takeover of my kitchen.

Bill said, "That's it. I'm getting ant poison."

Well, I hated using any poisons. Eviction is one thing, deterrence is fine; however, I have no capacity to poison any creature.

By midnight, exhausted and in despair at all my useless efforts, I sat on the floor in a corner of the kitchen. Then I concisely stated aloud to the endless gathering of ants marching across the floor and munching on our food and just lounging around that if they did not leave NOW, they would all die a miserable death by poison tomorrow. Sad and grim, I went to bed.

Next morning, I avoided the kitchen as long as I could. Finally I went in. No ants. No marching line. I pulled the cereal out of the cupboard. No ants swarming anywhere. Not one ant.

"Bill!" I shouted. "No ants!"

He examined the kitchen carefully, looking at me suspiciously as if he thought I had pulled a fast one, a sleight of hand. He finally agreed, no ants.

They never returned.

I thought a lot about what happened. Did the ants really hear me at some level? How and why did they all decide to vanish? Did they understand my intent? Was the entire colony connected as one entity?

This miracle of ant cooperation was, sadly, never repeated in my presence. Not long after we finished building our new home in Oregon, ants somehow breached our defensive building techniques. These large, half-black, half-orange ants completely ignored my efforts to banish them. They would deliver a stinging bite if you interfered with their freedom. Even the red-shafted flickers who ate ants like they were favorite jellybeans avoided these orange and black critters.

These ants were very good at reading intent, and hid quickly and completely before I was anywhere near them. Then they trotted blithely past me on their many feet when they somehow knew I was too busy to go after them.

Their invasion occurred in March. They scoured the house for something, but they weren't interested in our food items. I never saw them carrying any morsels. Perhaps they were searching for new sites to colonize. After a month or so, they retreated outside until the next March rolled around.

Though I maintained my habit of rescuing individual ants who fell into the birdbath, I dreaded their March return.

"Vacuum them up," suggested Bill, busy with his own work.

I did. The vacuum cleaner allowed me to eject them unharmed some distance from our house. I never knew if they got lost and never returned to their colony.

But, not surprisingly, vacuuming didn't cause even a blip in their numbers. One day, I found myself on the floor making a chosen victim run in circles by blocking any forward motion with a piece of cardboard. (Yes, I'm writing this during a March invasion.) Good thing no one could observe this woman the ants drove crazy.

My connection with ants was not easy to dismiss. On one of those occasionally really bad times that confront us all, I was despairing over events and choices that suddenly engulfed me. I escaped out into the woods. In a fog of depression, I kept on moving for hours, paying no attention to where I was. Finally, I collapsed in a small clearing. Although I didn't initially notice, I realized I was sitting on the ground next to an ant colony nest. Yes, the black and orange.

Mind a blank, I watched them coming and going. Some seemed to wander without direction near the colony nest. Inches from the nest site, I remained unmolested. The warrior ants, significantly larger, dominated the crowd. With so many ants bustling around it seemed impossible to keep track of any individual ant. But gradually I noticed a few small ants sort of aimlessly moving in circles. If they had been human I would have thought they were lost. A warrior ant rushed out of the ant mass carrying the carcass of some kind of insect. Instantly, two of the meanderers met the warrior, and the carcass was delicately transferred to them. They vanished into the colony nest.

A sense of calm washed over me at this bit of insight into ant dynamics. I continued to observe the busyness of the colony, and they continued to ignore me. No bites. I realized that, like the ant colony, I was part of a larger community, my input and effort as needed as everyone else's. We were all connected in mutual efforts not only to survive, but also to create an environment where we could flourish. The ants and all life-forms are a part of that.

Lately, I've been thinking about intention and belief and the inadvertent dance the ants and I got caught up in as a result. Intention and belief constantly fuel our human perceptions, our actions, and our decisions. Even intent alone is powerful beyond our own physical boundaries. For example, when someone intent on violence walks into a room, people respond with wary looks, by stepping away, or by feeling nebulous anxiety. I've seen this many times with many creatures. Though I have no proof, I suspect plants also have a version of this.

Micro-expressions and the cross-species' quick understanding of what is indicated by these expressions may play a role in the equally quick understanding of intent. But intent also works at a distance, while micro-expressions need closer range.

Ants will never give me the jolt of joy that seeing a horse racing free across the landscape does, or a dolphin leaping above the waves in exuberance, but they have changed my perceptions, clarified my intentions, and humbled my human arrogance. Not a bad day's work for ants.

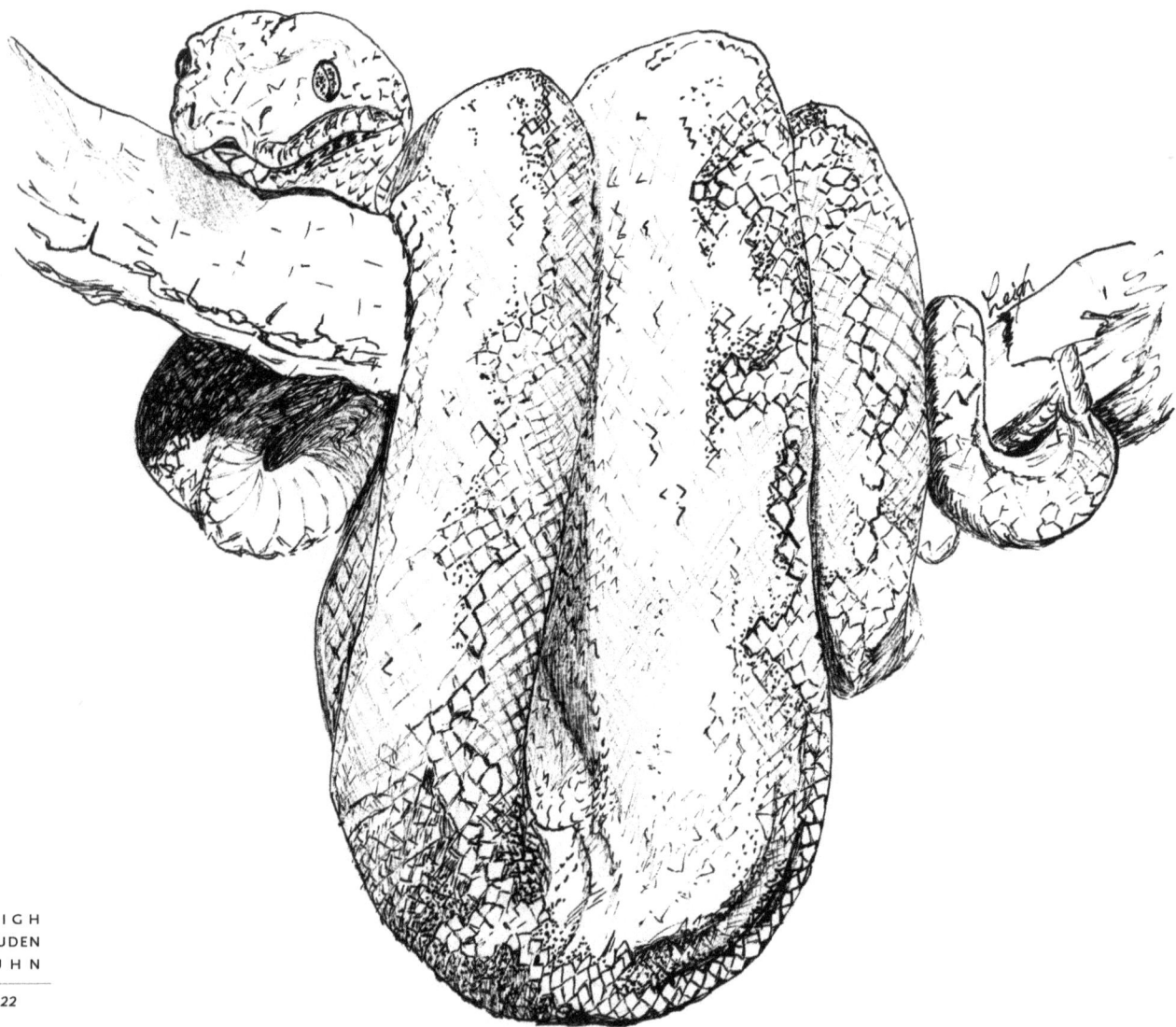

Chapter 6

Considerate Snakes

SOME KIND OF SNAKE LIVES IN ALMOST all the environments humans live in, so it is not surprising they appear in so many myths and legends. But all the depictions, characterizations, and treatments of snakes seem atavistic and intentionally negative. I've been wondering why since I was about ten years old.

I grew up along the east coast of Florida, where there were plenty of snakes to run into. Some of them were the most poisonous species in North America. I fearfully avoided them all and looked out where I was walking, especially in creek beds. No one ever had to tell me to BEWARE of snakes!

But children are ever curious and familiarity dulls caution. Eventually I was taken with the variety of designs and colors that decorated many of the snakes. It took a while, but I noticed that the colors and patterns of their designs matched the environment where I saw them, so they were very hard to spot unless they were moving. Whenever they started sliding through the grass or up a tree trunk, however, I got scared again.

On more than one occasion over the years since my early days in Florida, I accidentally stepped squarely on a snake. Almost certainly they were dozing on a warm spot before my foot came down upon them. Snakes are cold-blooded creatures, which basically means their bodies are not able to generate enough warmth to always function efficiently. So a sun-warmed rock can be necessary to a snake.

Once I stepped on a good-sized rattlesnake while exploring cliffs along the Mississippi River. My sister and mother were with me. My mother heard the telltale rattle of the snake but was too far away to react. My sister said later that I was silent and simply "levitated" a foot or so in the air. The snake oddly made no attempt to strike out at me. I was shaken but grateful.

If you bring up the subject of snakes in a conversation, the response is often an immediate expression of fear or repugnance. It is true that some snakes are dangerously poisonous, and a very few are so large and powerful they could squeeze someone to death, but the vast majority of snake species are not harmful to humans, and even the poisonous ones go to great lengths to avoid humans (thus the rare encounters). I've wondered if it is their manner of locomotion, having to wriggle everywhere on their bellies without benefit of hands, that causes us a sense of revulsion.

My snake encounters tended to be of the avoid-and-do-not-touch kind until my early twenties. I was living in northeastern Ohio, with a beautiful ravine full of hardwood trees as my backyard. One late autumn afternoon, I was perched at the edge of the ravine, the sun warm on my neck as the ravine cooled. I stretched out on my back and fell asleep.

When I awoke and sat up, a snake was curled in my lap. It was large enough that its tail curled back around my waist.

Very awake now, I recognized that this snake, familiar in the region, was not poisonous.

The moment was otherworldly. I felt no desire to dash the snake off my lap. It lifted its head and sent out an exploring forked tongue toward me, then laid its head back down on my knee.

I felt oddly at peace, even blessed, by what felt like a connection of some sort. The snake and I watched the ravine darken as the sun set. Then, calmly, after a last flick of the tongue, the snake glided off my lap and into the ravine, where it was instantly camouflaged into invisibility. I was left with a profound, undefined shift in my feelings regarding snakes, even the poisonous ones.

Since then I have unhesitatingly assisted snakes of many kinds across busy roadways, and have rescued a few being abused by humans. The abusers were each dragooned into an informative lecture about snakes and each had to apologize to the snake and then were allowed one gentle stroke while I held the snake. I did this with both adults and children. I've never had any pushback by snakes or people, and have never been bitten by a snake.

There was a resident snake at the nature center in Oregon where I worked. We named the snake Harry to help humanize him for visitors to the center. Harry was a hefty adult gopher snake, a.k.a. *Pituophis catenifer*. Gopher snakes are constrictors, which describes how they catch and subdue their dinner. I avoided ever watching this process, leaving the feeding part up to others while I did the talks and presentations.

Gopher snakes roam a huge and varied habitat throughout the United States and into parts of Canada and Mexico. If you have ever come across one, you may have easily mistaken it for a rattlesnake. Gopher snakes over time took on the coloring, patterns, and even the tail-shaking behavior of rattlesnakes. Even though the gopher snake does not actually have any rattles to shake and is not poisonous, this adaptation is useful in deterring enemies and avoiding attacks.

Over the roughly two years Harry and I worked together he offered me an encyclopedia of snake behavior information, but kept some of his mysteries to himself. I think one of them has to do with the forked tongue that snakes use to acquire a variety of necessary information. Their tongues have receptors that gauge temperature, scents, and sources of movement and vibrations. I believe there are many more unknown abilities linked to the snake's tongue receptors and nervous system, although I can't prove what they might be.

Harry harbored a dislike of men, even the ones who liked snakes. If an adult male fetched him from his roomy, glassed-in domicile, he would hiss and sometimes try to bite, which would hurt but not usually require first aid. He never exhibited those behaviors with women or children. It became routine to have whichever female employee or volunteer was available fetch Harry. How did he tell men from boys or women? Scent? Pheromones of some kind?

There were other subtle things I sometimes noticed him do or respond to that didn't fall into what his tongue was likely to perceive. Harry's mysteries.

Harry and I had a good relationship, meaning, at least, we were at ease with each other. From my perspective, it meant there was an element of trust present. Perhaps that stemmed from my experience with the ravine snake.

Sometimes our staff did snake presentations in venues away from the nature center. Harry traveled in a large velvet bag, but at the center whoever was giving the snake program usually transported him draped around the neck, shoulders, and arms. This method served to warm Harry up so he would be more active at our talks.

Despite his usual enigmatic demeanor, it seemed like he enjoyed these presentations. People responded to him with awe combined with various levels of anxiety. Harry would glide near the children who were entranced, but didn't approach the ones who were afraid, or whose parents were afraid.

How did he know? He responded to the few who wanted to touch him by remaining relaxed and still.

One late autumn afternoon at the nature center, I was alone, closing out the cash register with Harry draped artistically around my neck and shoulders and his head resting on my bicep. A well-dressed gentleman strode in, hoping to buy a gift for his daughter. He came over to the counter to pay and commented, "That's an amazing necklace and amulet – very realistic."

Thinking he was joking, I was about to reply when Harry abruptly tensed his muscles and lifted his head toward the man. At the same moment, I saw the man's face turn white. Both the unfortunate customer and I had an "oh no!" moment. He threw some money on the counter, turned, and literally ran out the door. Obviously not a snake fan.

I felt terrible. As a responsible employee, I should have put Harry back in his home earlier.

Harry swerved his head toward mine and danced his forked tongue gently down my cheek. It felt oddly like a reassuring pat on the back. I'd never seen him do anything similar before.

Having a wild snake choose to nap in my lap and the intimate, long-term situation with Harry were unanticipated gifts. I didn't realize then the impact these experiences would have on me over time. One of the most mind-opening realizations I gleaned was that snakes, like all life-forms, are unique individuals with unique personalities. Perhaps this is due to genetic quirks or glitches in DNA that play an important role in species survival, combined with gender differences, assigned roles, and individual environmental experiences. Or, perhaps it's just the way life on Earth works.

Snakes have been on Earth for well over one hundred million years, yet we know little of their complexities, physiognomy, and range of possibilities. Part of this is, I believe, due to our human biases that wall us off from truly exploring the myriad of unknowns.

Bill and Leigh at home in Oregon

Chapter 7

Home on the Range

THIS BOOK BEGINS WITH ANIMALS FOUND at home or close to it, and then moves – not always in a straight line; straight lines are rare in nature – farther from the house. Encountering truly wild animals is like stepping into another culture.

The standard view of domesticated animals is that they have no choice whether or not to have a relationship with us. They are subject to our purposes, desires, and restrictions. We also have imposed adaptations in many species, resulting in physical and behavioral changes and genetic alterations.

My mother once commented to me that humans can't help tinkering with everything. In the case of animals, the scope of tinkering has been profound and is ongoing.

Even so, the snake Harry at the Oregon nature center and the many birds of prey that were stars of the center's presentations somehow remained wild animals even in captivity. All of us who worked with them always held that understanding.

Let's consider coyote – not captive, but now frequently not far from humans. You may find my coyote experiences the most extraordinary parts of this book.

One night in Oregon when I heard their sounds – low growls and high haunting howls with little yips in between – I felt a combination of sorrow, elation, fear, and a call to action. I was supposed to do something. They were close, not far from our deck, throwing their untrackable voices into space. Life and death were colliding in my yard, thus my sorrow. The fear is an atavistic reaction; I'm not truly afraid. I wonder if the ants, lizards, and hibernating rodents also respond as I do, when they aren't the coyote's focus.

Just what was I supposed to do? Maybe it was to tell their stories.

Coyotes are now part of most terrains throughout our country and into Canada and Mexico. They pad through our towns, parks, cities, fields, mountain ranges, and deserts doing what their species is called to do, the call of the wild.

They are frequent visitors around our high desert home. Sometimes they are gone for weeks, then a solo coyote slides through the sage and bitterbrush. A flicker of beige or flash of a grayish ghost in a trot or lope they can maintain for hours.

Coyotes den and hunt alone, but their main social unit is a pair of adults that generally mate for life, which is good for them because, unlike domestic dogs, they have a very short window of time to produce pups each year.

Their fur ranges from beige to gray to reddish brown; their underbellies and the area under the throat are buffy or pale. Their guard hairs tend to have dark tips, and on their bushy tails near the top is a black patch that is the location of an important scent gland.

It's much easier to describe a coyote's appearance than it is to describe their essence and behaviors. They are in the canine family and can mate with other dog species, but any offspring can't reproduce. They flourish in packs or alone. Offspring can disperse on their own when they are about five months to a year old, or stay together with their parents and help raise a new generation.

No one knows the why of many of their behaviors, or the extent of their flexibility. I believe, though, that it is fundamental to their longevity as a species.

Coyotes seem to know when they are spotted by people, whether it is across a 75-yard field or on a quick dash through dense forest. They slow or stop and look over their shoulder right at you. How do they know we're watching?

I've never heard of a coyote attacking an adult human, but would imagine they might if cornered. The same cannot be said about us humans and our unending, unspeakable efforts to eradicate coyotes.

While coyotes, like domestic dogs, are omnivorous, and can subsist on just about anything organic, they have adapted strategies that enable them to include larger animals as prey. Unfortunately for them, this also puts them in direct conflict with humans, who rely on the same animals.

My sister Loren Cruden, in her book *The Spirit of Place*, wrote about coyotes as a totem to many of the Native American tribes. In her totem reference guide, she comments:

"In Coyote are all the so-called paradoxes of life; stories show this totem as both wise hero and silly fool. Coyote brings growth, transformation, reaching, testing – lessons we are often reluctant to face. Coyote teaches by humor, by example, by mirroring and reversal. This medicine brings rapid changes and expanded perception, which can be painful to the personal ego. Coyote is purposeful chaos."

Coyotes have many gradations of vocal sounds. On my first backpacking trip with Bill in Wyoming, I was excited by my introduction into wilderness mountain ranges. All the stoic granite mountainsides piercing their peaks into the clouds, and the clear quartz-lined streams interrupted by waterfalls, were my childhood imaginings made real.

I was also exhausted, struggling with a heavy backpack designed for long male spines, poorly broken-in boots (my own fault), and trying to catch my breath in such high altitudes.

Bill finally signaled a halt. Time to set up for the night, and eat dinner. I'd thought the running I did at home was enough preparation for this trip. I was quite wrong. My shoulders were bleeding under the straps of my pack and my feet were blistered. But the vast silence wooed me. As Bill fixed us a hot dinner, the tiny scrabbling of day animals finding their sleeping spots and the gurgle of the stream lifted my spirits.

Suddenly, a boom box turned up LOUD blasted through the quiet. It was playing the Beach Boys' old favorite "Help Me Rhonda."

I freaked out. "This is outrageous!"

Bill looked at me oddly. Then he commented, "Leigh, those are coyotes."

I still laugh when I remember this intro to coyote music. Sometimes when nearby coyotes sing to the moon I join in with "Help Me Rhonda" howls.

Chapter 8

Three Coyote Stories

I

ONE DAY IN YELLOWSTONE, ONE OF MY FAVORITE places to be, I was especially disposed to paying attention to its incredible beauty and diversity as I walked across a frost-sparkled field. Even so, I missed the swish of something moving in the tall grass until a coyote pulled up next to me. What's going on, I wondered, expecting her to recognize our mutual possibility of danger. I walked faster, ignoring her.

But she trotted along with me at just the correct distance that a "heel" command would elicit.

I looked at her, her face tilted up to read mine. We kept walking together. I wondered if somehow she was someone's pet coyote, or if she was high on peyote or some drug. I was getting nervous about the whole thing.

Once in a while, she would dash off to check on some possible prey, but then return quickly to my side. By then I was looking for ways to shoo her away.

We came upon one of the paved roads, and along came a car. I stopped at the road's edge to wave it down and ask for a ride. But it was already slowing to a halt next to me.

The coyote stayed right with me, sitting alertly – oh so well-behaved – and looking at the people in the car.

Before I could get a word out, the driver motioned to his wife to lower the window so he could speak, while the three kids in back gawked. He berated me for not having my dog on a leash, scolding me for how remiss I was for not considering the need to protect Yellowstone's wildlife. A bad example!

I looked at the coyote. Couldn't they see it was a wild animal? She stared up at me, seemingly adoringly. What I read in her golden, intelligent, laughing eyes was ... isn't this a marvelous joke!

The car drove off. The coyote stood up, still looking at me with a wide panting grin. Then she loped off into the woods across the road, never looking back, the trickster indeed.

2

ONE HOT JULY MIDMORNING, ABOUT halfway through my daily run, I collapsed under the shade of a huge ponderosa pine. Even my water bottle was on empty. Not good. I sat, head on my knees, eyes closed, a long way from home. Trees, brush, grasses, me – everything was weighted into stillness by the heat.

I heard a long sigh, and it wasn't mine. Sitting right next to me, almost haunch to hip, was a coyote.

I felt a jolt of shock, but only for an instant. That would send the wrong signal. For a while, I just looked at him out of the corner of my eye. He sighed again, looking at my face.

My sister and I are prone to talking to wildlife, especially when we don't have any better ideas to defuse anxiety. So I said, "What are you doing?"

Then, "Go away."

Then, more sternly, "Shoo ... shoo!"

He settled himself a few feet away with front legs stretched out.

I slowly got up and stepped out of the shade. Coyote got up, too, and did that bow that all dogs do when they want you to play. Front feet stretched out, rear end in the air, tail wagging, doggy grin.

"OK, I'm going now," I said.

He chose to accompany me down a deer trail, trotting, tail up, a few strides in front of me, until he spotted a rabbit scrambling away and took off after it. I don't know the rabbit's fate. I didn't want to think about it.

In retrospect, this coyote's behavior mirrored in many ways the behavior of ravens, crows, and dolphins. They are all known to create games, explore anomalies, and have a sense of humor that is recognized by others as humor.

What puzzled me about this particular experience and the Yellowstone coyote encounter is why the coyotes chose to play games with me. Maybe I needed a little more humor and some testing chaos in my life. Or perhaps they sensed I would get the joke.

3

OUR OREGON HOMEPLACE IS ALSO PURPOSELY a homeplace for wild-life, be they transient, seasonal, or residents. A few of them, I admit, are very undesirable, and these I try to encourage to find digs elsewhere. If they are repeatedly destructive to our house, we do our best to relocate them far away to sites appropriate to their needs (and where they won't get in trouble). This process is no easy task, and often I have mixed emotions about it.

Some of you may call this living with the wild, but it is much more nuanced than that. Yes, we've got lots of wildlife that have accommodated us living here, but the place functions in much the same way as a human neighborhood.

There is one feeder of black oil sunflower seeds for the birds. In return, they are very helpful in dealing with insect predators, so no pesticides needed. We have very gradually landscaped a small area around our house to augment what is naturally growing here, to help sustain the wildlife diversity in our transition zone. It is also tweaked to please our human aesthetics, and to provide some buffering against the wildfires that plague our state.

This includes additions of small ponds, a medium-small reflective pool, and a series of birdbaths strewn in various places. Water in the high desert is worth more than gold to people and wildlife alike.

The coyote in trouble is a case in point of our combined human/wildlife neighborhood.

A small deck extends across the front of our house, bordered by a narrow grass pathway and a native rock, herb, and shrub garden. This area holds several of the birdbaths.

One day I was finishing up watering everything when I felt someone close behind me. Not wanting to startle anyone, I slowly turned around. A coyote stood very close to my leg, watching me. It emanated tension and stress; its tail was tucked. I slowed and quieted my breathing. Saw no obvious injuries. No paws were lifted in pain.

My thoughts went to the possibility of rabies. I watched the coyote for any clues regarding its problem. It seemed to want my help, but I didn't feel like touching it. Now what?

The coyote looked around, dropped its head, didn't move. It was on the thin side but its fur was in good condition and clean. A distinctive marking across the shoulders and upper back looked just like a small saddle.

It seemed right to say quietly, "It's all right, you can be here." I filled a large saucer with water. If the coyote didn't drink or, worse, it actively avoided the water, I would go back to worrying about rabies, and my safety and that of the other animals.

It drank briefly and my stomach settled. Not rabies. I slid the saucer of water partway under the deck and sat on the deck, my back to the wall.

Coyote slowly crawled under the deck right beneath where I sat, hidden from casual view. After a while I leaned over to check. Coyote was curled up, dense tail wrapped around with only its eyes showing.

It was still there as evening shadowed the mountains. Some of the resident animals moved in close to the house, very aware of the coyote's presence. I thought they would warily stay away. One cottontail hopped right up and stared at the coyote. No movement but in the coyote's eyes. I was about to shoo the rabbit away when it started munching on nearby plants, still facing the coyote. Weird. What was that about? The rabbit hopped slowly away, unfazed.

I checked one last time, around midnight. The water dish was about half full and the coyote appeared more relaxed. The eyes acknowledged me. It was still curled up.

Next morning, it was gone. I found one pee spot but no tracks anywhere. The whole incident felt odd. The front deck area was business as usual so far as I could tell.

To me, the coyote's behavior spoke of a certain doggedness. This coyote was going to do this and make it work. Whatever was wrong with the coyote, apparently the coyote dealt with it.

The situation was not without risk. Most certainly, I would not necessarily recommend anyone do what I did, but the communication between us was clear, questions asked and answered. I confidently went with that.

This is not quite the end of the story. Nearly a month later, two young coyotes raced across our spot of lawn, right past me, playing and exploring in the rocks around the pond. They had the exact same saddle marking as on my mysterious one-day visitor. I've never seen any similar marking before or since, and I never saw the pups or the adult again.

Chapter 9

Grin and Bear It

I NEVER SAW A BEAR IN A ZOO OR IN THE WILD UNTIL I started high school in New York State. At the time, it wasn't clear to me if Yeti and Bigfoot were just versions of bears, all of whom I envisioned to be massive, smelly, grumpy, and inclined to kill you with one swat if you came across them with their offspring gamboling in tow. I knew bears hibernated in dens in winter and delivered their offspring during that time, but I wasn't sure this was believable. What kind of creature could sleep through delivering babies?

In fact, mama bears do arouse periodically to check on their cubs' needs, but at the time I imagined the poor tykes all on their own, waiting for their mother to finally wake up.

Bears in prehistoric times looked essentially the same as those currently wandering through North America, including in the Arctic region. The seemingly simple drawing of a cave bear on a cave wall in Spain some 40,800 years ago is amazingly accurate in form and full of bear essence ... alive.

The three kinds of common bears are black, grizzly, and polar bears. Those bears colored brown, cinnamon, and gray usually are *Ursus americanus* – the category of black bears.

Unlikely as it would seem by their size, black bears survive mainly on tiny foods: berries, nuts, inner tree bark, insects, and insect larvae. And honey – yes, like Winnie the Pooh. Once in a while, they may snatch up an unwary vole. Polar bears and grizzly bears, although technically omnivores, focus mainly on fish and a variety of animal prey – a good reason not to run into these bears.

We are not a friend or ally to bears. Historically, humans hunted bears for meat and fur and trophies, and killed them if they came too close to spaces claimed as ours. We have a well-deserved fear of bears and the havoc they can quickly rain down on us and the animals we protect.

Both the grizzly and the polar bear populations have been steeply declining in recent years. The rapid changes to our earth are already ahead of the polar bear's ability to adequately adapt, while loss of habitat drains the population of grizzly bears.

It was during those years in upstate New York that I saw vividly the juxtaposition of humans and bears. Our family spent several weeks each summer on Tupper Lake in the Adirondacks. I loved everything about being at Tupper. During our first visit there, my father talked about the bears. Black bears roamed through the Adirondacks, but there was one spot from which we could safely watch them. My father took us to the town garbage dump just before sunset.

Staying at a discreet distance upwind from the bears and the garbage odor, we saw an amazing sight. Perhaps two dozen bears rummaged through the dump. All the large ones were mama bears who kept close track of their pushing, playful, exploring cubs. Male bears live separate lives from their mates and offspring except for mating every other year.

What struck me was the sheer impact of their physical presence. Other than elephants, I've never been in the midst of such earth-connected power combined with speed and, disconcertingly, grace.

The watching humans were quiet, staying far enough away that the bears rarely had to send intimidating stares at any of us. It was obviously a common practice for bears and people to meet here at dusk. The cubs' little noises sounded almost like birds calling. The setting sun outlined the bears in hammered bronze.

"Time to go," my father whispered. It was then that a pervasive tension in the air struck me. Along with the tension, I was hit by a sense of something being wrong, and that both the people and the bears knew it. This was not how we should be living together.

My first up-close bear encounter was on a canoe trip in the northern reaches of Georgian Bay in Ontario, Canada. For our honeymoon Bill and I bought a canoe and some really dorky World War II army surplus hammocks, and then shoved off on a getting-to-know-each-other expedition for a couple of weeks. A bear encounter was not our only adventure.

On the map, we discovered an informal canal that looked like a good shortcut. It wended through tall grass and had rocky sides that almost touched us. A deep, helpful current drew us forward. I rested my bare feet on the metal deck covering the bow, now and then dipping my paddle to keep us on track. A large flat rock jutted into the channel at the next bend. Poised on the edge of the rock was a bear. He seemed as shocked as I was.

I tried to stutter "Bear!" to Bill but couldn't make my lips work. It appeared that the bear was in the midst of a well-used crossing point, baffled now as to how to proceed.

Standing upright, the bear extended one gigantic paw as if to step on the canoe's bow covering and deftly complete his crossing. But my bare feet were still propped there. In what felt like slow motion, the bear stepped backward with a disgruntled huff and retreated. The image of the bear, standing with raised furry paw right next to my bare foot, remained with me for years.

A FEW YEARS LATER AND A THOUSAND MILES to the west, Bill and I struggled to put up our tent in the middle of the night. Exhausted after an eighteen-hour road trip to the Wind River Range in Wyoming, we thought we were in one of the small clearings for tent campers. Good thing we were practiced at putting up our tent in the dark, pounding in stakes with our eyes practically shut. We shoved our sleeping bags and the next day's shoes inside and flopped down, already asleep.

Less than an hour later, the clearing around the tent was transformed into an elk thoroughfare replete with pounding hooves – and grunts and squeals when one or another elk tripped over a tent stake, snapping the tent flaps.

"Noooo ... I can't believe this," I wailed.

Finally the night grew silent. We slept.

Still in the bliss of sleep, I felt a very cold nose drift over my face, down my cheek, under my chin and back up. My groggy mind associated the cold nose with my childhood dog companion, Star. She used to wake me up in just such a manner.

"Go 'way," I grumbled. The icy nose began exploring my ear. I grabbed the muzzle and gave it a shake. "No, go 'way," I said sternly as I opened my eyes.

A thousand stars outlined a large teddy bear face a foot from mine. The bear hunkered at the tent entrance, but made no effort to enter further. OK. It seemed we both had decisions to make.

I whispered to my sleeping husband, "Bill, there is a bear in our tent."

No response. I said it again, softly, but with an underlying note of panic. "Turn on your other side and go to sleep," he said.

I rolled over with my sleeping bag over my face. I heard the bear move away. I slept. So ended my second encounter with a bear.

⟶

OVER THE YEARS, BEARS OCCASIONALLY roamed through my life, seeming unsurprised to see me. I acquired a sense of how they moved and what they paid particular attention to when they pointed muzzles a certain way. Except during mating season, the males deal with each other only as they tend to their carefully defined home boundaries, and search through their territory for the variety of edibles needed to successfully hibernate through winter. They tuck away honey, fat insects, berries, inner tree bark, and fish inside their dens.

The females keep to their smaller territories along with their offspring, who leave home by the end of their second year. Females avoid the adult males after mating season, partly to keep their cubs safe from attack from adult males. Preserving their territory is crucial for survival.

When they feel safe, bear families behave in ways that humans admire.

Cubs play, imitate their elders, invent games with which to challenge one another, and sometimes lie still, draped around mama bear. So much love, contentment, and joy, like a complex melody that is a constant background to their lives.

Whatever the reasons, the kingdom of the bears exists in a realm other than ours in spite of the occasional line-crossing by both bears and humans. These forays into more intimate relationships rarely end well for either party. Yet I think they are motivated by the fundamental desire for connections that seems to exist in most living things.

Bears allure humans with the shape of their bodies and faces. The bear sitting hunkered at the entrance to our tent, front paws splayed across each knee, presented an imitation of a hungry human waiting for his dinner plate. The wide forehead, wide-set eyes about the same size and shape and placement as ours, the short muzzle almost merging with the chin – all this was a cross between our beloved teddy and a slightly sly mirror of our own proportions.

None of these thoughts slid through my mind after the bear-in-the-tent incident though, until a time when I was employed calling for spotted owls in the trackless Cascade Mountains of central Oregon's old-growth forests.

One evening I also had to flag a trail before nightfall. Working my way along the trail I was marking, I paused, noticing a group of deer with spotted fawns standing as if frozen while looking down from the ridge above. I saw nothing to spook them into such odd stillness. I stopped, planting my foot on the decaying remnant of a huge old-growth tree. The remains of the bole were easily four feet wide.

On the far side of the downed tree the head and shoulders of a black bear emerged, grunting and huffing. The part of me that wasn't horrified noted how the setting sun turned the cinnamon tips of the bear's guard hairs into glinting treasure.

The bear was not a small one to be given a careless pat and goodbye.

It stood up, stretched a bit, and eyed my face with an occasional sniff. In a deja vu of the Canadian bear and our canoe, he put one back paw up near my foot on the tree trunk. I wanted to shriek and run but I remained as frozen as the deer. Then, for no particular reason, I stretched in parody, turned around, and began walking back over the faint trail I'd made.

Daring to glance back, I saw the bear had cleared the tree trunk and was following me. Oh, great. He fell into step just behind me, for a moment still on his back legs, still grunting and talking to himself. His breath was hot on my neck. I walked faster, trying out my own grunting cadence.

The trail fell on a gradual downhill to a stream. Abruptly, the bear veered off toward the water. I slowed to see where he was heading. Away from me, I hoped.

I waited. No more sign of him. The stream would drown out any sounds now. I could wait no longer. I burst into a flying run that would stun even

Usain Bolt. Still shaking, I leaped into my truck. It was another half hour before I was ready to call in my regular report. There was a long silence from my boss after he heard it.

—◆—

My last direct interaction with a bear was also the most intense. Bill and I were tent camping on a shore of Yellowstone Lake. Late September twilight purpled the lake's mirror of stillness. We chose a secluded picnic table on which to eat our pots-and-pans dinner, sitting in silence engendered by the coming night in such a huge landscape, and by our sadness at leaving Yellowstone the next day.

After a little quiet chitchat, I collected the pots and pans to wash them. It was almost dark as I swung one leg over the picnic bench and caught sight of a huge boulder a foot from the bench. I didn't remember the boulder being there. I held pots in one hand and used the other to grab the boulder for balance as I got up. It moved. Off balance, I grabbed again at the boulder and gripped a thick hank of fur. The boulder moved again. The only way to maintain my balance was to continue to hang on to what I quickly realized was a grizzly bear's neck. For me, time stopped.

The bear was mostly on all fours, busily checking out nearby vegetation. She lifted her head to give me a casual perusal while I remained glued to her neck.

I looked over at Bill. "What should I do?"

"Let go of the bear and drop the pots. NOW," he hissed.

I did, time started, and the bear gave me a last glance and continued her browse through the shrubs.

Science has tracking collars, cameras of all kinds, and other techniques to poke into bear dens and monitor bear matters, yet we know so little about the "why" of bears. You might also be pondering what bears really think of us.

Chapter 10

Look Closely

ONE DAY DURING MY WILDLIFE WORK in Oregon, driving home after a day cooped up in a conference room, I took advantage of the late afternoon light on the mountain peaks to stop and stretch my legs.

I started climbing up a steep hill bristling with tall grasses to get a good view. The grasses were dried into autumn gold. Near the top, my boot tromped on a thick rounded object that immediately twitched. I froze.

Yeah, a really sickening bad moment. How stupid of me to not watch my feet in rattlesnake country. No matter what I did next it was not likely to end well. So I did nothing.

About two feet from me a huge head rose slowly above the grass. A cougar's head, seemingly bigger than mine. Sleepy golden eyes glared at me. What to do, what to do. No wildlife manual covered this.

I lifted my booted foot off its tail, which was violently twitching, and earnestly told the cougar how really sorry I was, very sorry.

Then I drifted backward down the hill, never looking away. The visual details of the cougar became quite vivid in my mind.

The eyes were no longer sleepy and the cougar hissed at me. My two cats would have been envious.

I was watched the whole way as I backed down to my car, babbling apologies. The cougar never got up.

On these next pages are some other close looks that I drew earlier and now wish for time and energy to write about.

Flyers

Grouse

Barred owl

Hawk (Scottish buzzard)

Crow

Heron

Honey bee

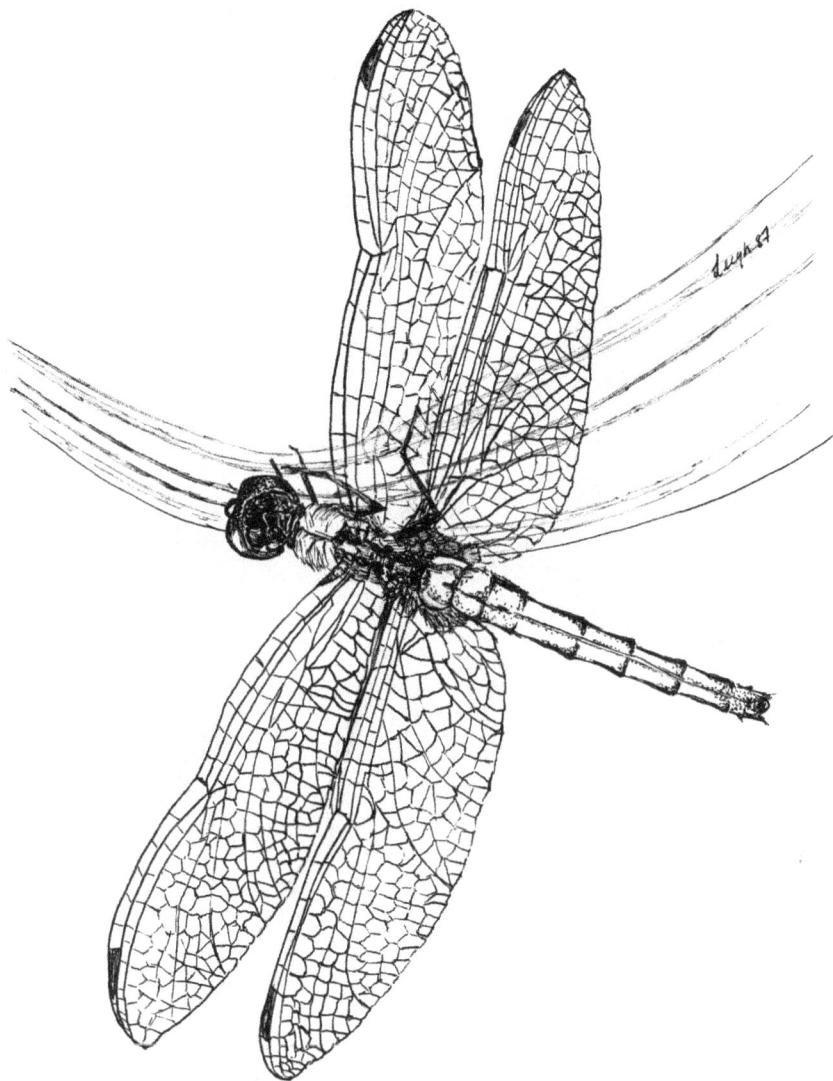

Dragonfly

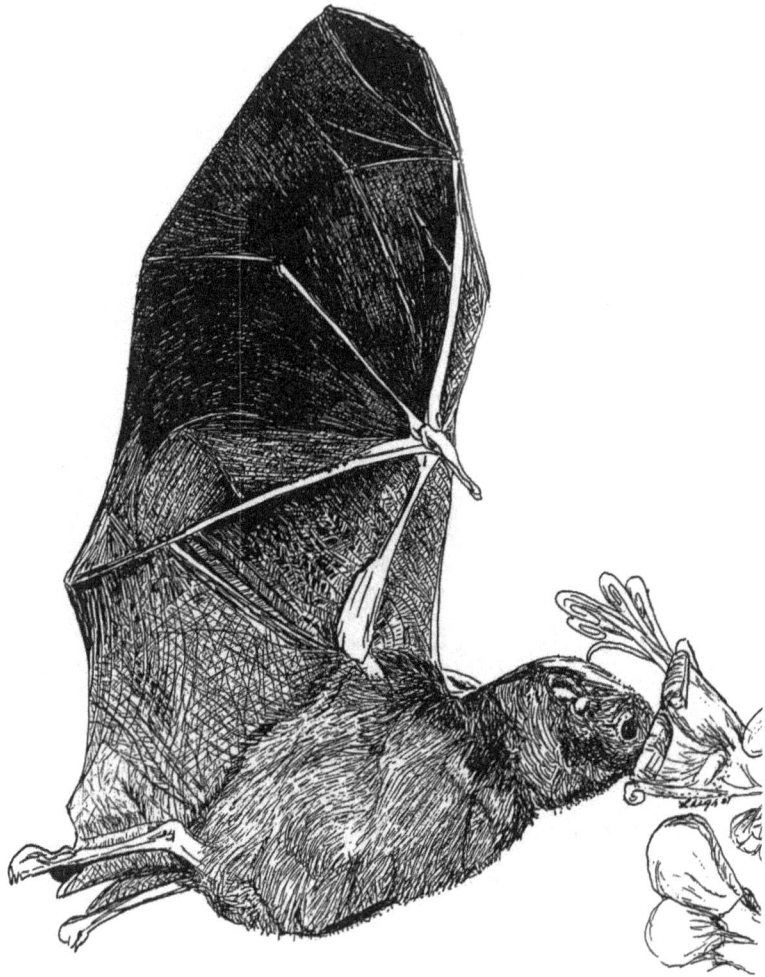

Bat

In the Water

Dolphins

Manatees

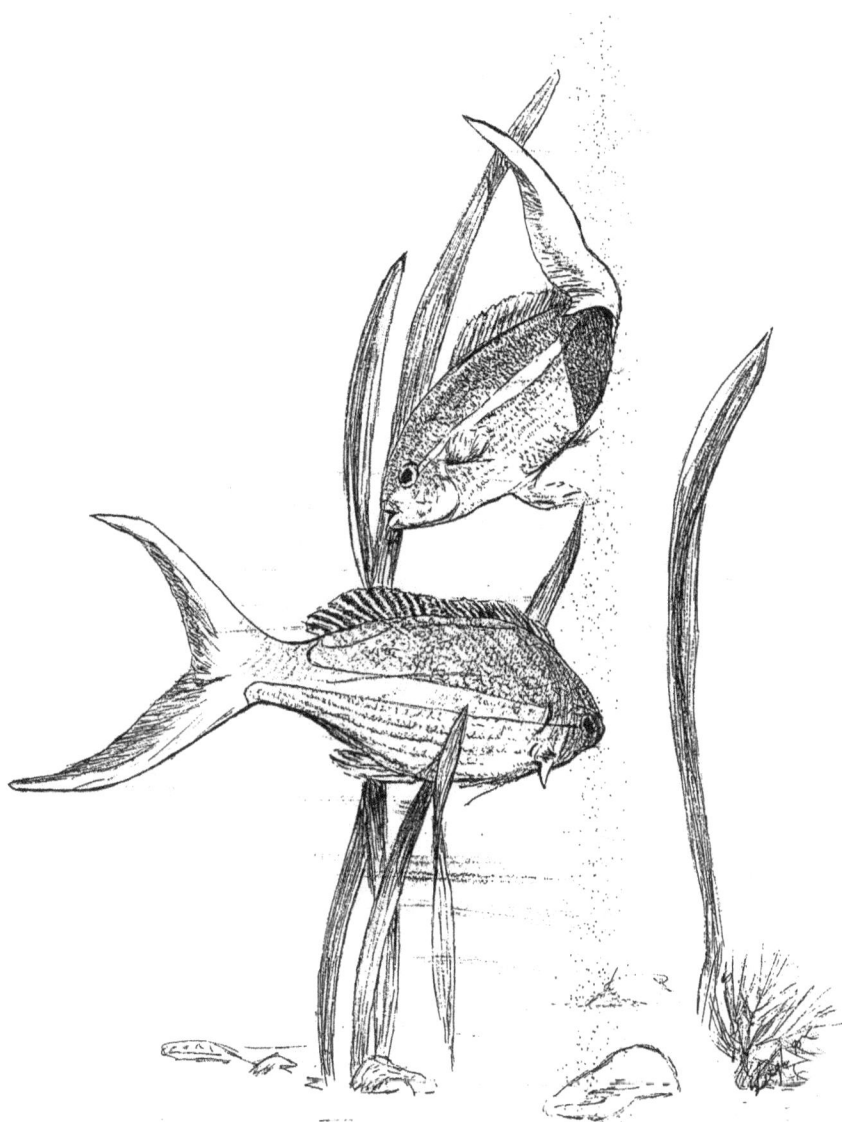

Fish

Salamander

Beaver

River otter

Seal

Dogs & Cats

German shepherd

Flubs, my sister's dog

Jumpers, my sister's cat

Two black Labs

Wild & Furry

Bobcat

Raccoon

Wolf

Bison

Deer

LEIGH
CRUDEN
KUHN

82

Boar

Prairie dogs

Wolverine

Weasel (Ermine)

Fisher

Woodchuck

Rats

Mice

Mole

Badger

Hare

Mountain goat

Tiger

Chapter 11

This Tree Is Whose Tree?

I WALK THE SAME TRAIL ALMOST EVERY DAY. I've done it for nearly a decade, and these four miles are like my husband's face in its myriad expressions, intimately familiar. The trail is also a journey of life in microcosm, with its landmark encounters and tracks of others here before me. Sometimes I play a passive role as observer, and sometimes I participate, willingly or not.

About a mile along the trail, a huge Ponderosa pine presides at a juncture in my route. It is easy to spot as a landmark when I occasionally wander too far off the trail. It's very old, very tall, and not the most attractive of its species. The sparse top branches scratch the desert blue sky. In spring and early summer, this tree is a popular hangout for the black-backed woodpecker. Chickadees, nuthatches, and occasionally sapsuckers perch on the branches, looking for a meal.

Four feet up its plated red-brown bore, the tree bulges like a full-term pregnant woman.

Sometimes I stop and put my ear to the bulge, wondering what the heartbeat of a tree sounds like. Maybe I can detect a sense of the flow of life up and down the chimney of cells under the bark.

Today, someone else crouches near the base of the tree.

"What's this?" I think, not pleasantly surprised. I'm used to being the only human on my route and I feel protective of the old tree.

A man is hammering a little metal plaque onto the crusty bark.

I try my pleasant lovely-day tone: "Hi, what are you doing?"

The man isn't fooled. "I'm not hurting the tree," he says.

I walk over, inspect the metal rectangle. It announces, BEARING TREE.

The man watches me read the marker. It explains that the U.S. Forest Service now owns this tree as part of a land exchange. It's been a bearing tree since 1863, as the man shows me on his map document.

How curious. I think about how this tree drew the attention of people almost 150 years ago as a landmark, a way to keep from being lost. Today it commands the same attention, and now officially so. The USFS thinks it owns this tree. Nope. The tree owns itself and gives whatever is needed to generations of birds, bugs, and humans.

A microcosm of life indeed. I step briskly down the trail. There will be new surprises and old faces. I still have miles to go.

Chapter 12

Parting Words

EVERY DAY, INDIVIDUAL ANIMALS, domestic and wild, present new mysteries, new lessons, and new connections through their humor, grief, strength, and compassion. If you pay conscious and thoughtful attention when you see other species that populate the earth, and consider the gifts of companionship, you too will participate in new ways.

Editor's Acknowledgments

My sister Leigh passed away September 15, 2016. This book was a late-life project we worked on together for as long as she could. If she were writing this paragraph she would have thanked her family deeply, as you no doubt guessed from reading this far. As you've similarly guessed from the many loving references to "Bill," she would have expressed particular and extensive gratitude to her husband, William Kuhn.

A person Leigh never met, Bridget Boland, brought a strong understanding and a wealth of improvements through her professional review of the manuscript. Her questions, sometimes challenging but always in service of the reader, cleared a natural path toward personal audience connection on many levels.

Book facilitator and family member Louise Hawker, proofreader Michele Siuda Jacques, and designer Thomas Osborne provided essential contributions.

Additional thanks occurred moment by moment through Leigh's life – thanks to each animal that accepted her curiosity and responded openly.

Alex Cruden

Tortoise

www.ingramcontent.com/pod-product-compliance
Lightning Source LLC
Chambersburg PA
CBHW080926050426
42334CB00055B/2797

* 9 7 8 0 6 9 2 1 0 8 0 9 3 *